Thank You!

I dedicate this book to my mother! I thank you for your continual encouragement and support in my life. Without you and your forever encouraging words, I wouldn't have been able to take a step in faith in overcoming my fears. I love you Ma!

Also, I would like to thank each kid this book reaches! This book is also dedicated to you because you all have inspired me to be able to tell my story while helping you overcome your fears as well. Remember, you can do it!

The Military Brat
The Experiences of Pooh New Faces

Title: The Military Brat
The Experiences of Pooh New Faces

Author: James "Pooh" Washington Jr

Description: This is the first book of the series The Military Brat, Experiences of Pooh. In this book, you will meet a child who faces early in life how to get over fears and dealing with being shy.

"New Faces"

Meet Pooh, the new kid in town whose father is in the military. Pooh wishes to go outside and play football with a group of kids from the neighborhood, but he has one problem! He is shy!!! Along with the help of his mother, see how Pooh is able to overcome his shyness inside!

Today is Pooh's first day living in a new state! Although he is used to moving around and making new friends he is a little nervous. Pooh is shy! Sitting at the window in his room, he sees a group of kids playing football in the neighborhood. Football is Pooh's favorite sport and he wants to go outside and play. Scared and not knowing what to do, his mother walks into the room to encourage him!

What's the matter, Pooh? Mom, I don't think I can go outside! Why not Pooh says his mother? Well, I'm nervous and what will they think of me? Am I good enough to play? Well, there's only one way to find out and I believe you can do it! You've always been fast and you can throw great. Okay mom, I think I can do it! You know what, says Pooh! You always give great advice mom!

Pooh runs to the bathroom, looks in the mirror, and quickly begins to doubt! Am I strong enough? Will they laugh at how I run? What if I can't throw far enough?

Suddenly, he remembers the encouraging words of his mother. He lifts his head and stares in the mirror! His heart beating like a drum, with a smile he whispers, "I can do it"!

Pooh runs out the bathroom! Not wanting Pooh to hurt himself, his mother yells out, "Slow it down before you fall". Yes mother Pooh responds!

He puts on his favorite red hat, looks out the window
one last time!

Runs downstairs, waves to his mother, takes a glance at the group of kids and proceeds to head outside.

Walking slowly towards the group of kids, Pooh notices that some are bigger, smaller, some are a different color than he, and also sees a girl. He has never seen girls play football! Continuing slowly, he walks up and introduces himself, "He guys, my name is Pooh". Quickly he hears, "do you want to play some football"? Relieved and with a big smile, he responds with, "of course".

He takes off his hat and runs on the field. Pooh is enjoying himself so much that he forgets he is shy. He even scores 2 touchdowns. Pooh and his new friends, play football all day long until the street lights come on.

While walking home, one of the kids yells, "Hey Pooh, same time, same place tomorrow alright". He gives the thumbs up and walks in the house.

Looks like somebody enjoyed himself and I'm so proud of you, says mom. You know what, I did and I scored two touchdowns responded Pooh. Mom, none of this would've happened if you hadn't encouraged me, explains Pooh. that's just another reason why God made us mothers, now let's shower as dinner is ready!

Pooh heads upstairs and walks in the bathroom! With his towel hanging over his shoulder, he looks in the mirror and whispers...

I did it!

The End...

Lets Talk About It:

What fears do you have and how can you overcome them?

Lets Talk About It:

What fears do you have and how can you overcome them?

Lets Talk About It:

What fears do you have and how can you overcome them?

Color With Me:

The Military Brat Pooh's Word Search:

```
Y  H  M  Z  A  B  N  U  R  E  X  Z  E  Z  V
R  O  N  O  Q  I  K  I  E  Z  V  N  T  S  A
A  O  O  W  T  W  X  W  B  S  C  A  S  N  B
T  P  G  Y  O  H  A  L  Q  O  J  C  R  D  Y
I  N  T  F  U  D  E  B  U  E  E  J  X  B  W
L  Q  U  D  O  O  H  R  O  B  H  G  I  E  N
I  M  Z  B  L  Z  A  C  C  V  Y  I  S  A  L
M  R  S  Z  V  G  W  D  U  S  Q  C  T  L  Q
S  O  N  H  E  L  F  C  R  O  A  P  A  H  J
O  T  K  M  Y  P  M  Q  B  R  T  B  I  V  I
O  F  E  U  M  K  D  G  E  T  T  R  W  H
H  N  L  E  W  O  T  D  A  O  J  F  S  U  G
T  M  B  S  I  W  I  R  O  A  G  P  S  N  H
J  D  B  G  W  T  B  F  R  I  E  N  D  S  F
E  I  W  V  Y  M  G  F  E  S  X  J  O  K  S
```

BRAT, BRAVE, ENCOURAGEMENT, FOOTBALL, FRIENDS, MILITARY, MOTHER, NEIGHBORHOOD, POOH, SCARED, SHY, SON, STAIRS, TOUCHDOWN, TOWEL

Color With Me:

Help Me Spell:
Fill in the blanks to finish the word

M_l_ta_y

P__h

_ootb__l

Mo_he_

En_ou_age_ent

Letter Bank:
i, r, o, f, a, l, t, c, m

You Can Do It...